JOSEPH

A MAN WITH CHARACTER

A SIX-WEEK BIBLE STUDY BY
RAND HUMMEL

Other Titles by Rand Hummel

Colossians: Jesus Christ—The Visible Icon of the Invisible God
The Dark Side of the Internet
Fear Not
Five Smooth Stones
God & I Time Treasures Volume 1 & 2
God is...Learning About My God
James: A Guidebook to Spiritual Maturity
Jonah's Magnificent God
Lest You Fall
New Testament Postcards
I Peter: Living in the Face of Ridicule
Philippians—The Secret of Outrageous, Contagious Joy!
Titus: Living a Christ-Centered Life in a Self-Centered World
Turn Away Wrath
What Does God Say About My Sin?

All Scripture is quoted from the Authorized King James Version.

Joseph: A Man With Character

Third Edition
A Six-week Bible Study
By Rand Hummel
Cover design by Craig Stouffer

© 2007, 2004, 2003 The Wilds Christian Association, Inc.
PO Box 509
Taylors, SC 29687
Phone: (864) 268-4760
Fax: (864) 292-0743

ISBN: 978-0-9829424-0-6

Joseph: A Man With Character

Genesis 37 – 50

Week 1: Joseph's Family Album

Monday: A Snapshot of Joseph's Father: Jacob
Tuesday: A Snapshot of Joseph's Mother: Rachel
Wednesday: A Snapshot of Joseph's Brother: Reuben
Thursday: A Snapshot of Joseph's Brothers: Simeon & Levi
Friday: A Snapshot of Joseph's Brother: Judah

Week 2: Joseph's Early Years

Monday: Tattletale or Truth-Teller
Tuesday: "Dad always liked you best!"
Wednesday: Dreamer of Dreams
Thursday: Sibling Rivalry at Its Worst
Friday: Obedience: Quickly, Sweetly, and Completely

Week 3: Joseph: Seventeen to Thirty

Monday: Joseph's Pit in the Desert
Tuesday: All Eyes Were on Joseph!
Wednesday: Let's Meet Poor, Pitiful Mrs. Potiphar!
Thursday: Joseph Faces Temptation Head-on!
Friday: Joseph Does Time in Prison!

Week 4: Joseph: A Leader in Egypt

Monday: The Cows and the Corn

Tuesday: Feast or Famine

Wednesday: Waking Up a Sleeping Conscience

Thursday: A Family Reunion

Friday: A Picture of True Forgiveness

Week 5: Joseph: A Type of Christ

Monday: Changed to Christlikeness - Part 1

Tuesday: Changed to Christlikeness - Part 2

Wednesday: Changed to Christlikeness - Part 3

Thursday: Changed to Christlikeness - Part 4

Friday: Changed to Christlikeness - Part 5

Week 6: A Review of Joseph's Life

Monday: Joseph's Family Album

Tuesday: Joseph's Early Years

Wednesday: Joseph: Seventeen to Thirty

Thursday: Joseph: A Leader in Egypt

Friday: Joseph: A Type of Christ

Introduction to Week One
Joseph's Family Album

Joseph was a teenager with character. Today we are surrounded with apathy, dishonesty, and compromise. Strong character is essential for spiritual success. As a teen, Joseph was hit in the face with hatred, mistreatment, lies, temptations, undeserved punishment, and gross misunderstanding. How did he handle all this? Joseph kept his focus on God and refused to get angry or bitter.

Godly character was as uncommon in Joseph's day as it is today. Our ultimate goal as Christians is to become just like Jesus Christ. God gives us many examples in Scripture that we can learn from to achieve Christlikeness or Christlike character. This week in our Bible study we are going to concentrate on Joseph's family and home situation. Good kids come from good homes or bad homes. The consistency of good parents gives us the desire to follow their examples of godliness and God-pleasing living. The consistency of wickedness in the home often develops a driving desire to be different in the heart of the teen. Either way, each one of us can be just as close to God as we want to be. There is no excuse to live a life without godly character. We all make independent choices every day. Joseph was definitely different than many of those in his family. Let's see what we can learn about how Joseph overcame a very difficult home situation. I trust this week's study gives each of you hope that regardless of your background you still can live a victorious, God-pleasing life.

A SNAPSHOT OF JOSEPH'S FATHER: JACOB
GENESIS 25 AND 27

Although Jacob had great faith, he was a disinterested dad. He did not get involved in the lives of his children! Jacob did not deal with his daughter Dinah's rape; he did not deal with Simeon and Levi's deceit and murder; he did not deal with Rueben's incest; and he did not deal with his sons' hatred and envy. Jacob was an impartial, unfair, disinterested dad...and the consequences were great.

Someone has categorized dads in four ways: neglectful, permissive, authoritarian, and biblical. Jacob was a mix of all four but leaned heavily on the neglectful side. Jacob was raised by a disinterested, neglectful dad and seemed to simply repeat how his father raised him. Who was Jacob's father? (Genesis 25:19)

_____

How old was Isaac when Jacob was born? (Genesis 25:26) _____

According to Genesis 25:27-28, did Isaac seem more interested in his first son, Esau, than he was with Jacob? _____

Why did Isaac seem to be interested in Esau but disinterested in Jacob? _____

_____

Jacob lived in a home where there was constant comparison. Describe the differences in looks, interests, and lifestyles between Jacob and Esau. (Genesis 25:24-34; 27:11-23)

_____

_____

Do you ever feel like your parents play favorites in your home? _____

_____

What does 2 Corinthians 10:12 say about comparing ourselves with others? _____

_____

Jacob probably felt like a nobody in his dad's eyes and that his dad really did not care about what was going on in his life. The problem was that he seemed to be just as disinterested in his own son's lives. Do we have to repeat the mistakes of our parents in our own lives? _____

_____

Do you think that when we stand before God He will listen to our excuse, "Well, that's just the way I was raised"? _____

_____

According to Romans 14:10-12 and 2 Corinthians 5:10, what will we be accountable for?

_____

_____

Jacob was also a man of great *fear*. His fear also could have kept him from being involved in his children's lives like he should have been. Read Genesis 32:6-7. Why do you think Jacob feared his brother Esau so much? _____

_____

What did Esau promise in Genesis 27:41-45? _____

_____

Who else did Jacob fear in Genesis 34:30? _____

Sometimes dads may seem confident and in control on the outside, but they face fears just like anybody else on the inside. If dads faced great disappointments and tragedies in their past, they may be afraid to open up and get involved in the lives of their kids or their wife. What do the following passages say about FEAR: FEAR about what others think, FEAR of losing those you love, and FEAR of failure or disappointment?

Proverbs 29:25 **The fear of man bringeth a snare: but whoso putteth his trust in the Lord shall be safe.**

_____

_____

2 Timothy 1:7 **For God hath not given us the spirit of fear; but of power, and of love, and of a sound mind.**

_____

_____

The third problem Jacob faced that could have fueled his disinterest in his sons was *guilt*. It is hard to deal with sin in others, even in your own children, when you have not dealt with that same sin in your own life! What does 1 John 1:9 promise to those who confess their sin? _____

_____

If we do not seek forgiveness from God and the ones we have sinned against, we will live in constant guilt and be too ashamed to confront those same sins in others' lives. What happened in Jacob's past with Esau that made it hard for him to deal with the hatred, anger, and jealousy between his sons and his wives? (Genesis 27) _____

_____

Jacob's sons lied to him and deceived him about Joseph's death. Can you remember a time when Jacob lied to and deceived his own father? What happened? (Genesis 27)

_____

Even though Joseph did not have a perfect role model as a father, he did not copy and repeat his father's mistakes. Joseph had the character to make choices that pleased God. Are you using a tough home situation as an excuse for not doing right? _____

_____

Like Joseph, you can be different. Strive to be like Christ rather than unlike one of your parents. Keep your focus on God, not others.

A SNAPSHOT OF JOSEPH'S MOTHER: RACHEL
GENESIS 29-30

Even though Rachel, Joseph's mother, had a precious son and a husband that loved her, she still struggled with discontentment. This is not uncommon even today. Many homes are filled with discontented kids, discontented dads, and discontented moms. Let's look closely at Rachel's life and see what God would have us to learn.

We first find Rachel in Genesis 29:6 as she brought her father's sheep to water at a well where Jacob had stopped on his journey. What did Jacob do to help Rachel in verse 10?

_____

According to verse 11, how did Jacob express his joy and thankfulness for God's leading him to his Uncle Laban?

_____

How was Jacob honoring his parents on this journey? (Read Genesis 28:6-7)

_____

Let's remember the customs of the time so we do not get sidetracked here and think it is biblical to kiss a girl on your first date. What did Jacob and Laban have in common with the way Jacob greeted Rachel and Laban greeted Jacob?

_____

There is a special joy when you know you are right in the middle of God's will. Jacob listened to his parents in his choice of a life mate while his brother, Esau, did not. According to Genesis 26:34-35, how did Isaac and Rebekah feel about the girl Esau chose to marry?

_____

It is very important that you honor your parents in your search for a life mate...even in the early stages.

From Genesis 29:16-17, describe the appearance of Leah and Rachel.

_____

According to Genesis 29:18, 20, and 30, describe Jacob's love for Rachel.

_____

Using Ephesians 5:25 and Colossians 3:19 and what we learned from Jacob's love for Rachel, explain how a husband today should love his wife.

_____
_____

Now Jacob had a problem. Because he did not follow God's example given to Adam and Eve, one wife for one husband, he was caught in a culturally acceptable situation that brought nothing but jealousy, hatred, and envy into his life. Even though Rachel had a husband who loved her very much, that was not enough. She thought she had to have more to be happy and content. What made Rachel so envious of her sister? (30:1)

___

You can see Leah's and Rachel's attitudes of jealousy, envy, and the way they fought for Jacob's love by the names they gave their children (or the children of their servant girls, which is another custom hard to understand). Read each verse and name meaning and try to imagine what Leah and Rachel were thinking as each child was born.

REUBEN: *see a son* (29:32) _____

SIMEON: *hearing* (29:33) _____

LEVI: *attached* (29:34) _____

JUDAH: *praise* (29:35) _____

DAN: *judge* (30:6) _____

NAPHTALI: *my wrestling* (30:8) _____

GAD: *to attack or invade as an army troop* (30:11) _____

ASHER: *happy* (30:13) _____

ISSACHAR: *he will bring a reward* (30:18) _____

ZEBULUN: *to dwell with* (30:20) _____

JOSEPH: *give me another* (30:22-24) _____

BENOMI: *sorrow* (35:16-18) _____

Because of Rachel's envy and discontent, she was not satisfied with just one son… she wanted more. God gave her one more son and then she died. She got what she wanted and still was filled with sorrow. Search your heart through the principles below to see if you have a discontented heart. Ask God to replace a discontented heart with a thankful heart.

Discontent Compares! "Look what they have!" 2 Corinthians 10:12

Discontent Complains! "I'll never enjoy that in my life!" Psalm 37:1-7

Discontent Criticizes! "It all comes so easy for them!" James 3:13-18

Discontent Craves! "I'll never be happy until I get everything I want!" Hebrews 13:5; Philippians 4:11; 1 Timothy 6:8

Joseph seemed to make the best out of every situation. Obviously he did not learn it from his discontented family. Remember, God has already given us everything we need for our present contentment. Never allow discontent to destroy a thankful heart. Be thankful today!

A SNAPSHOT OF JOSEPH'S BROTHER: REUBEN
GENESIS 29:32; 35:22; 37:21-26; 42:20-22; 49:1-4

Joseph's oldest brother was Reuben. As the firstborn son, Reuben was in line to become the leader of the entire nation of Israel. Read the passages in Genesis listed above to get a quick glimpse of his life.

In Genesis 49, we find Jacob on his deathbed leaving his sons with words of blessing and rebuke. Write out verses 3 and 4.

_____

_____

_____

Picture Jacob, about 147 years old and almost blind, sitting on the edge of his bed giving this blessing to Reuben.

Reuben, you are my first son. Your mother and I were so excited at your birth that all we could say is, "See, a son!" That's what your name, Reuben, means. You see, Jehovah God promised my father, Isaac, and my grandfather, Abraham, that we would have so many children, grandchildren, and great-grandchildren that you could not even count them…as many as the stars in the sky. You, Reuben, were the beginning of my might and my strength. You gave me hope…hope that God's promise was going to be fulfilled. Because you are my firstborn son, you are first in line to take over the family. You are to receive twice as much wealth in your inheritance than all your other brothers. You have an excellent position of power and authority. For years I was so proud of you. Reuben, you could have been a great leader…but you blew it…you stepped over the line. Reuben, let me describe your character…and the description of your character will be written in Jehovah God's book for all to see…Genesis 49:4 **Unstable as water, thou shalt not excel; because thou wentest up to thy father's bed; then defiledst thou it:** *(then turning to the other sons)* **he went up to my couch.**

What happened? Remember Bilhah, Rachel's servant girl and the mother of Dan and Naphtali? Rueben made a very wicked choice and slept with her. What we learn from Reuben's life is that he could have been a leader, but he chose to be a loser. Actually, there are three areas in Reuben's life where he was definitely a loser: he was a loser in the face of temptation, in the face of peer pressure, and in the face of his family. I trust that as you study this man's life, you will learn **not** to follow his example.

REUBEN COULD HAVE BEEN A LEADER, BUT HE CHOSE TO BE A LOSER.

1. **Reuben chose to be a loser in the face of temptation.** Read Genesis 35:19-22. What tragedy happened in Jacob's life? (35:19)

_____

What tragedy happened in Reuben's life? (35:22)

_____

The sin of immorality has great consequences. What three consequences does Proverbs 6:32-33 say come with adultery?

_____

_____

How did Joseph handle the same temptation in a very different way? (Genesis 39:7-10)

_____

_____

In a few words, what do the following verses say about our personal purity and how we should handle the sin of immorality?

1 Corinthians 6:15-20 _____

_____

1 Thessalonians 4:3-7 _____

_____

2. Reuben chose to be a loser in the face of peer pressure.

Read Genesis 37:17-36. Reuben did have his limits. But he chose to compromise rather than take a stand against his brothers. Read Genesis 37:21-22 again. He wanted to free Joseph from his hateful brothers and should have taken Joseph home to Jacob. Verse 21 says, **he heard it.** Reuben's brothers were not afraid to talk about their murderous plan in his presence. What do your friends talk about in your company?

Do your friends know that you love God and hate sin so much that you would do whatever you could to stop them?

_____

Reuben sought to live on the edge. In essence he was saying, "Let's not kill him and be personally guilty for his death; just throw him in a pit and he will die naturally!" Reuben wanted to keep Joseph from being killed, but he also wanted to fit in with his brothers. Is that how you live your life?

_____

Do you ever compromise with sin by thinking, "I'll go to the party, but I will not get involved. I'll dress like I am sexually involved, but I won't actually do it." What does Proverbs 1:10 say about peer pressure?

_____

3. Reuben chose to be a loser in the face of his family.

He let his little brother down and lied to his father causing great pain and heartache. Reuben didn't care how they felt. Do you care about your family?

_____

Does your attitude hurt your mom or dad? _____

Spiritually, do you help your brother or sister or hurt them? _____

Go back to Jacob's blessing in Genesis 49:4. He called Reuben **unstable as water** which is controlled by the temperature around it. Are you controlled by temptation, peer pressure, and selfishness?

_____

REUBEN COULD HAVE BEEN A LEADER, BUT HE CHOSE TO BE A LOSER.

A SNAPSHOT OF JOSEPH'S BROTHERS: SIMEON & LEVI
GENESIS 34:1-31; 49:5-7

Joseph had two very angry brothers: Simeon and Levi. Jacob described their selfish, angry character in Genesis 49:5-7 which reads,

> **Simeon and Levi are brethren; instruments of cruelty are in their habitations. O my soul, come not thou into their secret; unto their assembly, mine honour, be not thou united: for in their anger they slew a man, and in their selfwill they digged down a wall. Cursed be their anger, for it was fierce; and their wrath, for it was cruel: I will divide them in Jacob, and scatter them in Israel.**

At first glance, it seems that Simeon and Levi's anger against Shechem was justified. Read what happened in Genesis 34. Have you read it? Good! Simeon's and Levi's slaughter and spoil of the city was not a "righteous indignation" (a right kind of anger) but a violent and vengeful murder spree that was quite displeasing to Jacob and God. How do you handle your anger? Are you the kind that "blows up" or "clams up"?

_____

When was the last time you lost your temper? Who was it toward and what did you say or do that you wished you wouldn't have?

_____

Today we are going to look at several principles of selfish anger learned from Simeon and Levi in Genesis 49:5-7.

SELFISH ANGER LEADS TO VIOLENCE

Instruments of cruelty are in their habitations (49:5b).

This phrase means, "their swords are implements of violence." The instrument of cruelty is speaking about a **sword**. Because of what happened to their sister Dinah, these guys went crazy killing everyone in their path. There are many who are physically abused because of uncontrolled anger. What did Jesus imply was the root sin of murder in Matthew 5:21-22?

_____

Have you ever seen a brother or sister so mad they said, "I wish you were dead" or "I'm gonna kill you"? In Genesis 4:5-10, who was **wroth** or angry?

_____

Why was he so upset? _____

What was his brother's name? _____

What did he do to him? _____

Selfish anger, the kind that leads to violence and abuse, is sin.

SELFISH ANGER DRIVES LOVED ONES AWAY

O my soul, come not thou into their secret; unto their assembly, mine honour, be not thou united: (49:6a)

This actually means, "Let me not enter into their council or join in their assembly." In other words, "Because of their selfish anger, I do not respect what they have to say and I'm not going to hang out with them or join their group of friends." Write out Proverbs 22:24-25.

_____

_____

What could you learn if you became best friends with an angry person?

_____

Read what happened to Joseph's father in Genesis 27:41-45. What did Esau's anger cause Jacob to do?

_____

Do you like being around brothers, sisters, or even parents when they are angry?

_____

Do you think they like being around you when you are mad? _____

What needs to change in your life? _____

SELFISH ANGER ABOUNDS IN FOOLISHNESS AND CRUELTY

...for in their anger they slew a man, and in their selfwill they digged down a wall. Cursed be their anger, for it was fierce; and their wrath, for it was cruel: (49:6b-7a)

Angry people do things they would not normally do when they are not angry. Have you ever been so mad you said or did some things you wish you wouldn't have?

_____

Not only did these guys violently murder many people, the phrase **in their self will they digged down a wall** is better translated *they hamstrung oxen just because they wanted to*. These guys took their swords and cut the tendons in the back of the oxen's legs to lame them, just out of sheer meanness and cruelty! What does God say in the following verses about the foolishness of anger?

Job 5:2 _____

Proverbs 14:17 _____

Proverbs 14:29 _____

Proverbs 29:22 _____

Ecclesiastes 7:9 _____

SELFISH ANGER RESULTS IN TERRIBLE CONSEQUENCES

I will divide them in Jacob, and scatter them in Israel (49:7b).

God punished Simeon and Levi's family by never letting them own land to call their own. What does Proverbs 19:19 promise?

_____

We have seen three results of selfish anger. Ask God to protect you from following in Simeon and Levi's footsteps. Handle your anger God's way by confessing it to Him and the individuals involved.

A SNAPSHOT OF JOSEPH'S BROTHER: JUDAH
GENESIS 38:1-30

Joseph's older brother, Judah, really blew his testimony in his teen years and early twenties. Even though Joseph and Judah lived at the same time with the same father and knew about the same God, they made very different choices in regards to personal separation. Read the entire chapter of Genesis 38. It is interesting that God put this dark chapter right between chapter 37 where Joseph was bought by Potiphar and chapter 39 where Joseph was tempted by Mrs. Potiphar. Give two possible reasons why God placed this chapter where He did.

HINT NO. 1: (Compare the way Joseph and Judah handled temptation.)

_____

HINT NO. 2: (God's people were about to mix in with the Canaanite people.)

_____

Even as a young teen, Judah did not seem content to follow Jehovah, the God of his father, grandfather, and great-grandfather. How old do you think Judah was at the beginning of chapter 38?

_____

This will blow your mind, but Judah was probably around 14 years old when his first son, Er, was born, around 28 when his grandson, Perez, was born and about 43 when his great-grandson, Hezron, was born. (They started young in those days.) Even as a 14-year-old, rather than please God by keeping separate from unbelievers, he wanted to be liked and accepted by the people he lived around regardless of what they believed or how they lived. (Sound like anyone you know?)

According to Genesis 38:1, 12, and 20, who was Judah's best friend from the city of Adullam?

_____

From what you read in verse 20, did Hirah try to keep Judah from sinning or become a part of the attempted cover-up of the sin?

_____

What two qualifications of friends are mentioned in Psalm 119:63?

_____

Write the names of your three best friends. _____

Would you say they fear God and try to obey God's Word? _____

Do your best friends help you sin or help you stay away from sin? _____

In what ways can a friend help you stay away from sin? _____

_____

What do Proverbs 13:20 and 1 Corinthians 15:33 say about companions?_____

_____

If your best friends are unbelievers, it would be very easy to chose a wife that was also an unbeliever. We, of course, do not know Tamar's heart, but we do know that she was raised as a Canaanite with their culture and gods and she knew what a prostitute looked and acted like.

What was Judah's great-grandfather, Abraham, concerned about when it came time to find a wife for Isaac? (Genesis 24:1-4)

_____

According to Genesis 26:34-35 and 28:1-4, what were Isaac and Rebekah's thoughts on their sons marrying those who did not believe in Jehovah God?

_____

Write the principle found from Deuteronomy 7:2-4 in regards to marrying an unbeliever.

_____

Are you a Christian? _____

What does God say in 2 Corinthians 6:14-18 about who a Christian should marry?

_____

Study the following words and their meanings from 2 Corinthians 6 and match each of these five words with the proper application below.

FELLOWSHIP: *metochos: a sharer, a partnership, an associate or friend*

COMMUNION: *koinonia: fellowship, doing things together*

CONCORD: *sumphonesis: accordance, harmony, togetherness*

PART: meris: *to have in common, an inheritance to look forward to*

AGREEMENT: *sugkatathesis: thinking alike, in accord with, no friction*

1. Without _____ there will be no eternal inheritance together: one will spend eternity in heaven and the other in hell.

2. Without _____ there is constant discord and friction: no harmony.

3. Without _____ there will be no close fellowship or doing things together as a loving couple.

4. Without _____ there is no strong companionship or friendship: they will not share the joy of living together as best friends.

5. Without _____ there will be constant disagreement and arguing.

According to Jacob's final words of blessing on Judah, we assume that Judah had a change of heart in his later years and sought to know and please God. God does forgive, but the consequences of sin are great.

What kind of son was Judah's first son, Er, and what did God have to do to him? (Genesis 38:7) _____

Before Judah was 35 years old, what happened to his wife? (38:12)

_____

Judah suffered great heartache because he chose to live like the world and refused to be separate from unbelievers. What does God want from us today? _____

Saturday and Sunday Review

Today and tomorrow, go back to each day's study and slowly re-read each question and answer. After reading and meditating on each day's principles, in the spaces provided write out what you learned from them and how you want God to use it to help you have the character and integrity of Joseph.

Monday

A Snapshot of Joseph's Father: Jacob
Genesis 25 and 27

_____

_____

_____

_____

_____

_____

_____

_____

_____

Tuesday

A Snapshot of Joseph's Mother: Rachel
Genesis 29-30

_____

_____

_____

_____

_____

_____

_____

_____

_____

A SNAPSHOT OF JOSEPH'S BROTHER: REUBEN
GENESIS 29:32; 35:22; 37:21-26; 42:20-22; 49:1-4

_____

_____

_____

_____

_____

_____

THURSDAY

A SNAPSHOT OF JOSEPH'S BROTHERS: SIMEON & LEVI
GENESIS 34:1-31; 49:5-7

_____

_____

_____

_____

_____

FRIDAY

A SNAPSHOT OF JOSEPH'S BROTHER: JUDAH
GENESIS 38:1-30

_____

_____

_____

_____

_____

_____

_____

Introduction to Week Two
Joseph's Early Years

Joseph was a 17-year-old with character. Genesis 37 is filled with some of the problems Joseph faced as a young man. He not only was surrounded by envy, hatred, and jealousy, he had just lost his mother. It is tough for any teen to watch a parent die. It seemed that as much as his father loved him, his brothers hated him. He was in a no-win situation with his older brothers. It was quite obvious that his father loved him more than his other brothers and was grooming him to take over the family. You see, his other brothers had disqualified themselves to rule the family. Reuben was immoral with Bilhah, Simeon and Levi in anger went on a murder spree, and Judah chose to mix in with the Canaanites and be like them. Joseph seemed to be the only one that had a heart for God. Not only did Jacob see this, but God did also. God spoke to Joseph through dreams just as He did to the Patriarchs before him: Abraham, Isaac, and Jacob. God and Jacob had special plans for Joseph. But his brothers had other ideas. Because of their hatred and jealousy, they simply wanted to do away with Joseph, thus doing away with the notion that he would someday rule over them.

Tattletale or Truth-Teller
Genesis 37

And Jacob dwelt in the land wherein his father was a stranger, in the land of Canaan. These are the generations (this is the history) of Jacob. Joseph, being seventeen years old, was feeding the flock with his brethren; and the lad was with the sons of Bilhah, and with the sons of Zilpah, his father's wives: and Joseph brought unto his father their evil report. Genesis 37:1-2

Let's look at what Scripture tells us of Joseph as a kid. Joseph is first seen in Genesis 30:22-24. In this passage, what is implied about Rachel in verse 22?

God "hearkened" or listened to her.

Although Rachel struggled with discontent, she must have prayed. How important is it for us to pray about our burdens?

When and where do you pray each day? _____

Genesis 33:1-7 is the second time we find Joseph. Jacob is afraid that Esau may follow through with his threat of killing Jacob. Why do you think Jacob lined up his family the way he did in Genesis 33:1-7?

It could be that Joseph and Rachel were considered Jacob's most prize possessions, so he gave them premium protection. What we prize in life is what we protect, guard, and are willing to fight for. What is the most important thing in your life?

The third mention of Joseph is his name in a list with his brothers in Genesis 35:24. What happened to Joseph's mother right before this? (Genesis 35:16-20)

Joseph got a little brother and lost a mother on the same day. It's tough to grow up, especially without a mom. Do you know anyone whose mom has already died?

How could you be an encouragement to them?

The fourth mention of Joseph is Genesis 37:1-2. Nobody wants to be called a tattletale—they have a way of getting us into trouble. There are two very different approaches to Genesis 37:1-2. Either Joseph was simply giving the facts and telling his dad what was going on or he was selfishly trying to get his brothers into trouble. (By the way, if we don't do anything bad, then we cannot be tattled on.)

What is the difference between telling someone who can help and malicious gossip?

Nobody wants to be a "narc"…although, if we got rid of all narcs, we would have a whole lot more drug-related crime and tragedies. Some teens, in an attempt to have a godly school or youth group, are pegged as undercover cops or secret agents. That's too bad. Allowing a nest of poisonous snakes to make themselves at home in your group is crazy.

A commentator named John Butler gives us a few questions to ask in trying to decide where Joseph was coming from.

1. Who did Joseph talk to? _____

He told only the one who needed to know in order to stop the problem. Who do "gossips" tell? _____

2. What did Joseph say? _____

Did he tell the truth or make it all up? _____

(By the way, if gossips were limited to just the facts, they would not have many juicy things to say.)

3. Why did Joseph speak? _____

If he was simply trying to get his brothers into trouble then he would be a tattletale. If he really wanted to help his brothers to stop their wickedness then he would be considered a truth-teller! The last time you "told on" someone, was it to help them or to get them in trouble?

_____

Based on the three questions above, write three principles that show the difference between tattling and honestly trying to help.

1. _____

2. _____

3. _____

What do the verses below have to say about gossip and truth telling?

Proverbs 11:3 _____

_____

Proverbs 18:8 _____

_____

Proverbs 27:5-6 _____

_____

Proverbs 28:23 _____

_____

2 Thessalonians 3:14-15 _____

_____

"Tattletales" seek to get others in trouble. "Truth-Tellers" want to help those who are destroying their own lives with sin. Whether or not Jacob asked for the report does not really matter. When we see someone involved in behavior that will ultimately hurt them and others, we need to love them enough to confront them with the evil.

"DAD ALWAYS LIKED YOU BEST!"
GENESIS 37

Now Israel loved Joseph more than all his children, because he was the son of his old age: and he made him a coat of many colors. And when his brethren saw that their father loved him more than all his brethren, they hated him, and could not speak peaceably unto him. Genesis 37:3-4

Everybody loves to be loved and likes to be liked. When you feel that someone does not like you and likes one of your friends or even your brother or sister more than you…it hurts! In Genesis 37:3-4, Joseph's brothers HATED him and couldn't even talk nice to him just because his father showed favoritism towards him. It wasn't Joseph's fault. There could be a couple of reasons why Jacob did show favor towards Joseph.

1. Joseph was the waited for and prayed for son of Rachel, his true love.

2. Joseph was a comfort to his 91-year-old dad and spent time with him.

3. Joseph refused to put up with the evil wickedness of his brothers.

4. Some Bible teachers say that **the son of his old age** is a Hebrew phrase for a wise son, one who possessed wisdom above his years, an old head on young shoulders. From the four reasons above, all of which commend Joseph, which of the four could be said about you?

_____

Remember, a holy, respectful, unselfish attitude will always be honored and esteemed over a proud, rebellious, selfish attitude. Regardless of WHY Jacob loved Joseph so much, nobody wants to be constantly compared with others. Playing favorites is not just a parent problem, it is amazing how many kids and teens play favorites with their friends and family. In the space below, write out 2 Corinthians 10:12.

_____

_____

Comparisons cannot be made without experiencing acceptance or rejection. The fear of rejection is a morbid fear—knowing that the one person who should love you, chooses not to, because we cannot meet up to his or her expectations. So we give up, quit trying, and rebel against that standard that we feel we could never achieve anyway. Who do you know that thinks you look down on them or don't like them?

_____

Gossipping and talking behind another friend's back is often centered around comparisons. List four ways that you or your friends compare others in your life. (I'll give you a hint on the first one.)

1. *the way others look* _____

2. _____

3. _____

4. _____

Who made you? _____ Who made your friends? _____ Who gave us the looks that we have? _____ Who gave us the talents that we have? _____ Who gave us the abilities that we have? _____ So when we attack the way someone looks or acts, who are we actually attacking? _____

What do the following verses say about how God gives different gifts and abilities to different people?

1 Corinthians 12:11 _____

Romans 12:6 _____

1 Corinthians 7:7 _____

What does the last phrase of Genesis 37:4 say about the way Joseph's brothers talked with him?

_____

Do you talk mean to your brothers or sisters? _____

Do you have friends at school or church that could accuse you of not liking them and being rude to them?

_____

What does Ephesians 4:29, 31, and 32 say about how we should talk to each other?

_____

Ephesians 4:29 speaks of corrupt, rotten, cut-you-down kind of words.

Explain how arguing and fighting are corrupt. _____

_____

Explain how sassing and talking back to parents are corrupt. _____

_____

Explain how making fun of and cutting down are corrupt. _____

_____

God loves us with an UNCONDITIONAL LOVE. He loved us while we were yet sinners. God does not play favorites. Read the verses below and comment on how God does not respect one person above another.

John 3:15-17 _____

_____

Romans 2:11 _____

_____

1 Peter 1:17 _____

_____

God loves us with an unconditional love—no strings attached. He does not love us by the way we look or the abilities we have. He just loves us! And we should do the same for others. Don't play favorites!

DREAMER OF DREAMS
GENESIS 37:5-11

And Joseph dreamed a dream, and he told it his brethren: and they hated him yet the more. And he said unto them, Hear, I pray you, this dream which I have dreamed: For, behold, we were binding sheaves in the field, and, lo, my sheaf arose, and also stood upright; and, behold, your sheaves stood round about, and made obeisance to my sheaf. And his brethren said to him, Shalt thou indeed reign over us? or shalt thou indeed have dominion over us? And they hated him yet the more for his dreams, and for his words. And he dreamed yet another dream, and told it his brethren, and said, Behold, I have dreamed a dream more; and, behold, the sun and the moon and the eleven stars made obeisance to me. And he told it to his father, and to his brethren: and his father rebuked him, and said unto him, What is this dream that thou hast dreamed? Shall I and thy mother and thy brethren indeed come to bow down ourselves to thee to the earth? And his brethren envied him; but his father observed the saying. Genesis 37:5-11

Dreams and visions were God's way of speaking to His believers before He gave His written Word, the Bible. God spoke to and through the Patriarchs—men God chose to lead His people. The first was Abraham. God spoke to him, encouraging him to leave his homeland and head for Canaan, the land promised to his descendents. (Genesis 12) Isaac was next. God spoke to him warning him not to go to Egypt during a famine. (Genesis 26) Jacob was the third Patriarch. God called him Israel after they wrestled. (Genesis 28:12) Now we have God speaking to Joseph. God put His hand of approval on Joseph giving him a glimpse of his future rule over his family which may have been a promise that kept Joseph from giving up through the years of slavery and prison.

How does God speak to us today?_____

When and where do you sit down and let God speak to you each day?

_____

Have you ever read the Bible through from Genesis to Revelation? _____

God's Word has specific answers to specific questions and problems.

Where would you read if you want to learn about true love? _____

Where would you read if you want to understand true joy? _____

Where would you read if you want to study the tongue? _____

Where would you read to understand assurance of salvation? _____

(Choose from: 1 John • Philippians • James 3 • 1 Corinthians 13)

Have you ever wished that God would tell us what to do by writing it in big letters in the sky or telling us in a dream? Actually, we have it much better than how God spoke in Joseph's day. Match the phrases on the next page.

1. _____ The Bible is more detailed than dreams because…

2. _____ The Bible is more trustworthy than dreams because…

3. _____ The Bible is more authoritative than dreams because…

4. _____ The Bible is more certain than a dream because…

A. …we use the Bible to check the dream, not vise versa.

B. …dreams can be forgotten or vague in time. The Bible is complete and right before us.

C. …only the dreamer knows the dream and therefore it is impossible to examine. The Bible is open for all of us to search and study.

D. …it covers more subjects. Dreams are limited.

In verse 8 of today's text, we see that Joseph's brothers hated him because the dreams revealed that he would rule over them. Joseph took a stand against sin and wickedness and his brothers did not want an authority that would keep them from doing what they wanted to do.

Do you know any teachers who kids hate because they enforce the rules? _____

What do rebellious friends think of other teens who try to respect authority and obey the rules?

_____

Have you ever been hated because you took a stand for what was right? _____

What do the following verses say about being hated by wicked men?

Matthew 5:11-12 _____

Luke 6:22 _____

John 15:18 _____

1 John 3:13 _____

The last verse of our text today, verse 11, says that Joseph's brothers envied him because of his dreams. What is envy?

_____

When you are jealous or envious of someone else's looks, talents, friends, or things, what does that envy say about your heart?

_____

What does God say about envy in the verses below?

Proverbs 14:30 _____

James 3:13-18 _____

1 Peter 2:1-3 _____

God revealed His future plan to Joseph through his dreams. Joseph accepted it as truth and trusted God that it would happen. Let's do the same with God's Word every day of our lives. Simply trust God's Word!

THURSDAY

SIBLING RIVALRY AT ITS WORST
GENESIS 37

For review and today's study, read the entire chapter of Genesis 37 again. Yesterday we caught a glimpse of the hatred and envy Joseph's brothers had towards him because of his dreams. Today we will refocus on the incredible <u>sibling rivalry</u> that took place in this ancient family.

List the reference where we find these attitudes and actions among Joseph's brothers.

Joseph's brothers hated him. _____

Joseph's brothers spoke harshly to him. _____

Joseph's brothers hated him more and more. _____

Joseph's brothers envied him. _____

Joseph's brothers conspired to kill him. _____

Joseph's brothers roughly threw him into a pit. _____

Joseph's brothers didn't care (ate while Joseph suffered). _____

Joseph's brothers sold him as a slave. _____

Joseph's brothers lied to their father causing great grief. _____

Joseph's brothers pretended to comfort their dad. _____

Joseph's brothers were content to watch their dad grieve. _____

Define what the world calls <u>sibling rivalry</u>. _____

_____

List the names of your brothers and sisters. _____

_____

When was the last time you had an argument or a fight with a brother or sister?

_____

Do you feel in competition with any of them? _____

It almost seems accepted in most homes today for brothers and sisters to be at each other's throats. Our family members should never be our rivals! Most who graduate from high school and go off to college leave home with many regrets, one of which is memories of constant fighting and contention. Your brother or sister <u>should</u> be one of your best friends. Let's look at a bunch of Scripture passages that deal with this issue of <u>sibling rivalry</u>. Before we start, stop and pray and ask God to show you anything in your life that needs to change in this area.

Contention is a fancy word for argument, conflict, or strife. Where does Proverbs 13:10 say contention starts?_____

Describe how a proud person argues._____

_____

If there is an argument between you and a brother or sister, what does this verse say is true about one or both of you?

_____

Read Ephesians 4:29-32. What kind of language should never come out of our mouths? (vs. 29)

_____

The word corrupt means to make rotten or to ruin. How can harsh, unkind words hurt our relationship with a brother or a sister?

_____

The word edifying means to build up, brag on, uplift. When was the last time you made one of your siblings feel better because you built them up and bragged on them?

_____

God put verse 30 right in the middle of this passage for a reason. When we are unkind towards one another, what does this do to the Spirit of God?

_____

What six things do we need to put away (get rid of) according to verse 31?

_____

Read verse 32 again. How has God been kind, tenderhearted, and forgiving to you?

_____

In what way can you be the same towards your brother or sister? _____

_____

What does James 4:1 say is the main reason for strife? _____

In the previous chapter, in James 3:14-16, when there is envying and strife in your hearts, what three words in verse 15 describe this kind of wisdom?

_____

What two results does verse 16 say will be in your home?

_____

Now read James 3:16-17. What seven characteristics of godly wisdom—the wisdom that is in total opposition to sibling rivalry—are listed in verse 17?

_____

_____

Looking at these two types of wisdom, which one most describes you and your relationship with your brothers and sisters: the peaceable, godly wisdom or the earthly, unspiritual, demonic wisdom?

_____

If strife, contention, arguing, and fighting is epidemic in your home, ask God to take away the driving desire in you to change your brothers and sisters, and give you an intense passion to change yourself. God was not pleased with sibling rivalry in Joseph's day…and He is still against it today.

OBEDIENCE: QUICKLY, SWEETLY, AND COMPLETELY
GENESIS 37:12-17

And his brethren went to feed their father's flock in Shechem. And Israel said unto Joseph, Do not thy brethren feed the flock in Shechem? Come, and I will send thee unto them. And he said to him, Here am I. And he said to him, Go, I pray thee, see whether it be well with thy brethren, and well with the flocks; and bring me word again. So he sent him out of the vale of Hebron, and he came to Shechem. And a certain man found him, and, behold, he was wandering in the field: and the man asked him, saying, What seekest thou? And he said, I seek my brethren: tell me, I pray thee, where they feed their flocks. And the man said, They are departed hence; for I heard them say, Let us go to Dothan. And Joseph went after his brethren, and found him in Dothan. Genesis 37:12-17

Joseph's family were shepherd nomads who had to travel to find good grass and water for their flock. The sheep were their livelihood, and it seemed as if Joseph's brothers had much more concern about their sheep than their own brother. Even today, many families put "things" over family relationships and then, when the material things have fallen apart or gone out of style, they end up with absolutely nothing at all.

When Jacob asked Joseph to go and check on his brothers, what was Joseph's three word response to his father? (vs. 13)

_____

Some translate the words **Here am I** either "I will go" or "Very well." Joseph was quick to obey…no excuses…no complaints…no griping…just simple, quick, and complete obedience. Joseph could have said…

"But Dad, do you realize how far of a walk that is? Almost 60 miles!"

"But Dad, it's too hot! It'll take me a couple of days and what about food, water, and what if someone comes after me and tries to rob me?"

"But Dad, don't you remember what Levi and Simeon did in Shechem? And you want me to go all by myself?"

"But Dad, my brothers hate me! Please don't make me go to them. They might get so angry that they will slap me around or beat me up!"

"But Dad …!"

List three excuses you have used with your folks in the place of quick, sweet, and complete obedience. _____

_____

Write out the classic verse on obedience of children. Ephesians_____

_____

What does Ephesians 6:2 say? _____

_____

Write out Colossians 3:20. _____

_____

When it says, **Children, obey your parents,** it simply means quick, instant obedience. Which phrase in the verses above refers to a respectful, sweet attitude?

_____

_____

Which phrase in the verses above refers to "complete" obedience?

_____

From these three principles, we can get a good, clear explanation of true obedience. How are we to obey?

QUICKLY, SWEETLY, AND COMPLETELY

Before you started first grade you would probably have said, "Quickwee, Sweetwee, and Compweetwe." Regardless of how you say it, it must become a part of your life. Explain why it is sometimes hard to obey quickly.

_____

_____

Explain the difference between obeying with a "sweet" attitude and a "not-so-sweet" attitude.

_____

How would the principle of "complete" obedience affect the way you clean your room, help clean up the kitchen, or respect a curfew set by your parents?

_____

_____

What is the 5th commandment of the ten commandments in Exodus 20?

_____

What does Proverbs 6:20 teach? _____

_____

Read Deuteronomy 11:26-28. What does God give **if ye obey**? _____

What does God promise **if ye will not obey**? _____

Explain how teenagers who obey quickly, sweetly, and completely can be a blessing to their parents, to their teachers, and to their employers.

_____

Now explain how disobedience, or even compliance with a rotten attitude, can cause great heartache and grief at home, at school, at church, or at work.

_____

_____

If you learn to obey quickly, sweetly, and completely as a child or teenager, then when you are faced with God's commands in your life as an adult, you can, with confidence, obey God…**QUICKLY, SWEETLY, AND COMPLETELY.**

Saturday and Sunday Review

Today and tomorrow, go back to each day's study and slowly re-read each question and answer. After reading and meditating on each day's principles, in the spaces provided write out what you learned and how you want God to use it to help you have the character and integrity of Joseph.

Monday

Tattletale or Truth-Teller
Genesis 37

_____

_____

_____

_____

_____

_____

_____

_____

Tuesday

"Dad always liked you best!"
Genesis 37

_____

_____

_____

_____

_____

_____

_____

DREAMER OF DREAMS
GENESIS 37:5-11

_____
_____
_____
_____
_____
_____
_____

THURSDAY

SIBLING RIVALRY AT ITS WORST
GENESIS 37

_____
_____
_____
_____
_____
_____
_____

FRIDAY

OBEDIENCE: QUICKLY, SWEETLY, AND COMPLETELY
GENESIS 37:12-17

_____
_____
_____
_____
_____
_____
_____

Introduction to Week Three
Joseph: Seventeen to Thirty

Joseph could never be accused of having it easy or being sheltered from pain and suffering. He wanted to do right. Between the ages of 17 and 30 his reward for doing right was more rejection and hurt. Whether thrown in a pit or a prison, Joseph kept his integrity by keeping a strong focus on the promises of God. Living a life that attempts to please God is not the best way to win any popularity contest. Joseph was consumed with and committed to pleasing God. That commitment kept him from giving in to total despair during the tough times he faced that absolutely made no sense. Because Joseph did not give up or give in, the 13-year trial from age 17 to 30 ended in over 70 years of blessing.

What trials are you currently facing that make no sense at this time? Do you ever feel that the more you try to do right and please God, the more difficult it is to face family and friends? You may not actually be thrown into a prison cell, but the rejection, the misunderstanding, the hatred, the lack of concern by almost everyone is a prison sentence in itself. This week we will see how Joseph hung on and made it through 13 very difficult years.

JOSEPH'S PIT IN THE DESERT
GENESIS 37:13-35

Read Genesis 37:13-35. Did you read it? Great! Joseph obeyed his father without question. What he did not know was that when he left to check on his brothers, he would not see his father again for almost thirteen years. What did Joseph's brothers do when they saw him coming across the field towards them? (vs. 18)

What did they call Joseph in verse 19 that hints at why they hated him so much?

What did these guys think they would accomplish by killing Joseph? (vs. 20)

Who gave Joseph his dreams?

Did Joseph's dreams ever come true?

How does God speak to us today?

Will the promises and warnings in the Bible ever come true?

List two Bible promises and two Bible warnings that affect your daily choices in life.

Wicked men, not understanding the power of the Word of God, think that they can do away with God's influence by doing away with those who have chosen to live for God. Even the public burning of early church martyrs only inflamed the hearts of hundreds more to give their lives for God. In Joseph's day, they decided that the best way to thwart God's plan was to kill God's man. Today, many teens seek to do away with God's influence by getting God's man to join their wickedness. Maybe these sons tried to get Joseph on their side against Jacob, but he would have nothing to do with disloyalty and dishonor to his father. Either way, the same drive in the hearts of Joseph's brothers is seen in the hearts of so many God-haters today as they will do whatever is possible to get rid of the convicting, godly influence in their lives.

From today's verses, whose idea was it to throw Joseph into a desert pit?

What was Reuben's secret plan? (vs. 22)

Unless Reuben could rescue Joseph from his brothers, this pit was actually a death sentence. With the drought-like conditions of the desert, these pits would attract all kinds of animals seeking water, but once in the pit, they could not get out. Often there would be a great stench from the rotting flesh of water-seeking animals. No water…no way out… sure, slow, agonizing death for Joseph—whose crime was that he represented his father's love and his Heavenly Father's will. What is the worst thing that has ever happened to you because you refused to join in with others' sin and took a stand for what is right?

As we know, God was with Joseph and not only helped him out of this pit, but also years later, took him to a magnificent palace. Joseph may have been thrown into a physical pit, but his brothers were caught in a spiritual "pit" of sin. What is the last phrase of Genesis 37:27?

The boys were content to kill Joseph…content to let him die in the pit…and now content to send him to a life often worse than death that often resulted in death—the life of a slave. How content are you with sin: very content, kind of content, or seldom content?

Most of us would never be content to murder someone, but there are all kinds of sins that we allow ourselves to become very comfortable with. Without writing it down, what sin is such a major part of your thinking that it does not seem to bother you anymore? In other words, what sin have you simply learned to be content with? Below are four ways to become content with sin.

1. **Surround yourselves with others who are content with sin.**
   (*And Judah said unto his brethren…*)

2. **Judge sin by its pleasure now…not its punishment later.**
   (*What profit is it if we slay our brother?*)

3. **Convince yourself that it is okay, as long as you don't get caught. Have a good cover-up plan.**
   (*… and conceal his blood.*)

4. **Harden your heart to the distress your sin causes others.**
   (*… and the brethren were content.*)

Through God's sovereignty Joseph was lifted out of his desert pit and sold into Egypt. Through God's strength each one of us can be lifted out of our prison-like pit of sin. If you feel you are caught in a hole so deep that you cannot get out, remember these promises from God's Word.

> **I waited patiently for the LORD; and He inclined unto me, and heard my cry. He brought me up also out of an horrible pit, out of the miry clay, and set my feet upon a rock, and established my goings. And He hath put a new song in my mouth, even praise unto our God: many shall see it, and fear, and shall trust in the LORD. Blessed is that man that maketh the LORD his trust.** Psalm 40:1-4

ALL EYES WERE ON JOSEPH!
GENESIS 39:1-23

Read the entire chapter of Genesis 39. Have you ever felt that everyone was staring at you? Most of us have experienced that uncomfortable feeling and wondered if we did something stupid or there was something hanging from our nose. Not many like the feeling of being watched. When Joseph was sold as a slave to Potiphar, the chief executioner in Egypt, all eyes were on Joseph. He was being watched! He was being watched by Potiphar; he was being watched by the other servants in the house; he was being watched by Potiphar's wife; and he was being watched by God. According the Genesis 39:3, what two things did Potiphar see about Joseph and his Lord?

_____

_____

_____

When our actions and attitudes draw attention to us, what do people see?

_____

Who do you know, teen or adult, about whom you could say, "They really walk with the Lord. God's blessing is so evident in their lives."

_____

What do others see in someone that reveals that God is with them and blessing their lives?

_____

List a few things a boss or employer might observe that would NOT reveal that God's blessing was on that life.

_____

_____

Now, do your authorities see God in your life?_____ People who have a good work ethic, who do not complain, and who try to do their best will be given much greater privileges and responsibilities. From Genesis 39:4-6, what kind of responsibility did Potiphar give Joseph?

_____

_____

Write out Ephesians 6:5-7 and explain how those verses should impact each one of us.

_____

_____

_____

Potiphar was not the only one watching Joseph; so was his wife! She continually tempted him to sin but he consistently refused. We will look at that situation more closely in our study tomorrow.

What three words in verse 7 tell us that Joseph's tempter was watching?

What phrase in 1 Peter 5:8 tells us our tempter is watching us?

What does 1 Peter 5:9 tell us to do?

Not only were Potiphar and his wife watching Joseph, but also Potiphar's servants were! Neither the trust Potiphar gave Joseph nor the temptations Mrs. Potiphar threw his way could go unnoticed by the other servants in the house. Whether Joseph's fellow servants respected him or resented him for getting a higher position, they couldn't help but see God's hand in his life. If one of your friends at work, school, or church were asked who they know that really has a heart for God and walks close to Him, would they give your name?

Why would they or why wouldn't they?

What principles in 1 Peter 2:15 and Titus 2:8 teach us how to keep a right testimony with our peers?

Not only were Potiphar, his wife, and his servants watching Joseph, so was God! We must **welcome** God's presence! The fact that God was with Joseph gives us a good idea about Joseph's heart…he wanted God with him! However, most people today want just the opposite; they do not want God in textbooks, in schools, in graduations, or even in Christmas! The problem is, God will give them what they want. If someone does not want God's presence, He will not give it. Write out James 4:6-8 below with these truths in mind.

Genesis 39:2-3 tells us God made Joseph to **prosper**. Define prosperity.

True prosperity is not in things or positions, but simply doing our daily duties in an excellent way that pleases God. To end our study, read and meditate on the following passages and thank God for keeping an eye on us at all times.

2 CHRONICLES 16:9 · JOB 34:21 · PROVERBS 5:21 · JEREMIAH 23:24

LET'S MEET POOR, PITIFUL MRS. POTIPHAR!
GENESIS 39:6-23

Read the passage listed above. This is all we know about Potiphar's wife, but it is enough to know that she was a wicked woman, the kind of woman we need to stay away from. Today in our Bible study, let's study some of the characteristics and thinking that is involved in a person who is continually looking to sin. Meet poor, pitiful Mrs. Potiphar.

1. MRS. POTIPHAR HAD AN IMPRESSIVE POSITION. She had everything that it takes to impress others…popularity, position, possessions, and power…but nothing to impress God. What is most important in your life—what others say about you or what God knows about you? Do you think you have fallen into the same trap as Mrs. Potiphar in trying to impress friends with popularity or things? _____

When you shop for clothes, do you choose clothes that will get the attention of others and violate modesty or communication principles? _____

Write out Galatians 1:10 and explain how important it is to realize that we have no one to impress and only One to please. _____

_____

_____

2. MRS. POTIPHAR HAD A WANDERING EYE! Never think that what we allow ourselves to gaze upon is powerless in our thoughts and actions. Genesis 39:7 says, **his master's wife cast her eyes upon Joseph.** Just like Eve, Lot, Samson, and David, Mrs. Potiphar did not control what entered her eye-gate. What does Psalm 101:3 say about what we choose to look at?_____

_____

On a scale of 1 to 10, how well do you control your eyes? _____

How has television and the Internet been used by the devil to attack Christians regarding the "lust of the eyes"? _____

_____

According to 1 John 2:15-17 and Psalm 119:36-37, what should we pray?

_____

_____

_____

3. MRS. POTIPHAR HAD A LUSTFUL HEART. She actually asked Joseph to be immoral with her as she said, **Lie with me.** (39:7) What word is found in all three passages: 1 Timothy 6:11, 2 Timothy 2:22, and 1 Corinthians 6:18? _____

Mrs. Potiphar was a wicked woman. What did Joseph do that Mrs. Potiphar refused to do? (39:12) _____

_____

A **lustful heart** begins with a filthy mind. Write a short application of the following verses that deal with our thought lives.

Philippians 4:8 _____

_____

2 Corinthians 10:5_____

_____

Psalm 19:14_____

_____

4. MRS. POTIPHAR HAD A STUBBORN WILL. SHE WOULD NOT LISTEN TO REASON.
Others may have been caught in her web, but all of a sudden a young, good looking servant is standing up to her by simply saying, "NO!" He not only refused to sin, but also he tried to get her to change her ways. But she still refused to listen. Is there any area of your life where stubbornness stands in the way of reason? _____

What does God call **stubbornness** in 1 Samuel 15:23? _____

5. MRS. POTIPHAR HAD A DISRESPECTFUL ATTITUDE TOWARDS HER HUSBAND.
This is seen in verse 14. **That she called unto the men of her house, and spake unto them, saying, See, he hath brought in an Hebrew unto us to mock us;** Potiphar's wife quickly shifted the blame to her husband, showing great disrespect. What does Ephesians 5:33 teach young wives? _____

What usually happens in a home where the mom refuses to submit and is disrespectful to her husband? _____

_____

6. MRS. POTIPHAR HAD A LYING TONGUE! SHE COULD NOT BE TRUSTED!
It seems as if no one truly believed her. If the chief executioner's wife had truly experienced attempted rape, Joseph would have lost his head. Instead, he was put in prison, and given leadership opportunity even there. From Proverbs 12:22, what does God think about lying?_____

_____

7. MRS. POTIPHAR IS FORGOTTEN!
Some, through faith, will live forever. Others will cease to exist as soon as they are forgotten. What will be remembered about you when you leave your school?_____

_____

What will be remembered about you when you die?_____

_____

Let's learn from Joseph and not from Mrs. Potiphar.

JOSEPH FACES TEMPTATION HEAD-ON!
GENESIS 39:6-23

Read Genesis 39:6-23. It is amazing that each time we read through this passage, we learn something new. Joseph refused to sin with Potiphar's wife. Joseph kept his purity. How? Why? What was in Joseph's thinking and lifestyle that kept him pure? Can we stay just as pure in the wicked world we live in? These are all great questions which we will try to answer in today's study of Joseph.

Joseph faced intense temptation. Mrs. Potiphar did not hint or suggest; it was an all-out, in-your-face temptation when she said, **Lie with me!** When was the last time you faced such an intense temptation? Keep in mind, temptation is not sin, but yielding to the temptation is sin.

Joseph faced constant temptation. What three words in Genesis 39:10 show us that this temptation kept coming back on a daily basis? _____

Joseph knew he would have to fight temptation when he went to work! He had to be prepared ahead of time to say "NO!" Remember, Joseph could have done what most do today and made all kinds of excuses why it would be okay to sin. Like…

"No one will ever know. She wouldn't dare tell and jeopardize her position."

"Everyone else in my position would do it, so why shouldn't I?"

"Just one time to get her off my back; one time is no big deal."

"I'll get special privileges and extra pay by giving in."

"Wait a minute! I'm her slave. She owns me. I don't have a choice!"

"I might lose my job—maybe my head—if I say 'no'!"

Without writing it down, what is your favorite excuse when you face temptation? No one can make us sin. When anyone sins, they CHOOSE to sin. Not even the devil can MAKE us sin!

HOW DID JOSEPH REFUSE TO SIN?

And it came to pass, as she spake to Joseph day by day, that he hearkened not unto her, to lie by her, or to be with her. Genesis 39:10

He refused to listen to her! The phrase, he hearkened not to her, simply means he refused to listen to her. He would not let her talk him into sinning. Write out Proverbs 1:10.

_____

_____

According to Psalm 1:1, how does the man blessed by God deal with the ungodly, the scornful, and the sinners?

_____

He stayed away from her! The phrase, **or to be with her**, implies that he kept away from Mrs. Potiphar and her influence. Who usually talks teens into sin…a friend? Who introduces teens to drinking, smoking, drugs, or immorality…a friend? Do you have

40

any friends that try to talk you into getting involved in sin? If you have friends that constantly try to get you into sin, stay away from them! What do the following verses say about a Christian's choice in the friends they hang out with?

Proverbs 1:11-16 _____

Proverbs 4:14-15 _____

Proverbs 13:20 _____

2 Corinthians 6:14-17 _____

Why did Joseph refuse to sin?

But he refused, and said unto his master's wife, Behold, my master wotteth not what is with me in the house, and he hath committed all that he hath to my hand; there is none greater in this house than I; neither hath he kept back any thing from me but thee, because thou art his wife: how then can I do this great wickedness, and sin against God? Genesis 39:8-9

From these two verses we see three principles Joseph chose to believe and live by. Every time we are tempted to sin, we should boldly write these three principles on the chalkboards of our minds.

"Behold my master..."
I'll DISAPPOINT others that look up to me!

"...thou art his wife"
I'll DEFILE you. Don't ruin your life like this!

"...and sin against God"
I'll DISPLEASE God!

Think of three individuals who would be greatly disappointed if you turned your back on God and chose to live a life of sin.

You cannot help your friends by joining in on their sin. Is there anyone you need to apologize to because you made sinful choices in the past?

Is God more real to you than anything on earth? When temptation moves in, do you concentrate on the presence of a true and living God?

JOSEPH DOES TIME IN PRISON!
GENESIS 39:20-40:23

Read the account of Joseph's prison time in Genesis 39:20-40:23. Modern prisons are bad enough today, but they pale in comparison with the ancient prisons of Egypt. It seemed as if Joseph was punished for doing right, but God, in His sovereign plan, used 13 difficult years to prepare Joseph for 80 years of service.

Even though we do not admit it at the time, God knows what He is doing all the time. Humanly speaking, Joseph was a prime candidate for bitterness. Joseph refused to **fail of the grace of God**. You may feel like you are in "solitary confinement" from your friends and loved ones or you may have been misunderstood and mistreated through abuse, neglect, or forgetfulness and think that "NOBODY CARES, SO WHY SHOULD I?" Your spiritual success is not based on what others have done to you, but on your response to what has been done to you.

Let's learn from Joseph: the guy who refused to be bitter! Joseph's RESPONSE to his prison sentence is an example to us, proving that God's GRACE is always sufficient. Read through the outline below to get a good grasp on Joseph's prison time.

1. Joseph's response to the PRISON GUARD...TOTAL SUBMISSION! (39:21)

2. Joseph's response to the PRISONERS...TOLERANCE! (39:22)

3. Joseph's response to the PRESENCE OF GOD...TRUST! (39:23)

4. Joseph's response to POTIPHAR...OBEDIENCE! (40:1-2)

5. Joseph's response to PHARAOH'S OFFICERS...COMPASSION! (40:4)

   a. He **served them**. (He learned of the customs, idiosyncrasies, and secrets of Pharaoh and palace life!)

   b. He saw that **they were sad**. (He was looking!)

   c. He **spoke the truth in love**.

6. Joseph's response to his PAST LIFE...ENDURANCE! (40:14-15)

   a. He knew life was unfair. He refused to allow it to affect his choices as a godly servant.

   b. He did not use his tough situation as an excuse to sin.

   c. He continued to have HOPE. He never gave up!

Joseph describes his prison as a ward or a dungeon. Many believe his prison was a round structure such as a fortress—cold, dark, and damp—often below the ground level. The horror of prison life is almost indescribable with words. From the words used to describe Joseph's prison time, describe in your own words what it must have been like living in those miserable conditions in prison.

> prison...king's prisoners...bound...keeper of the prison...Pharaoh was wroth... house of the captain of the guard (chief executioner)...bring me out of this house... dungeon...forgotten...two full years...in ward (cage)...out of the dungeon... he shaved himself...changed his raiment...

_____

_____

_____

_____

Who does Genesis 39:21 and 23 say was with Joseph even while he was in prison?

_____

The presence of God can make a prison a palace, or a palace a prison: depending on your relationship with God. Read Genesis 40:1-4. What does verse 4 say Joseph did to the butler and the baker?

_____

_____

We are never more Christlike than when we serve. One writer said, "God has three sorts of servants in the world: some are slaves, and serve Him from fear; others are hirelings, and serve for wages; and the last are sons, who serve because they love."

How do you serve? _____

Who do you presently serve in your life? _____

_____

List some of the acts of service you have done for others in the last three weeks.

_____

_____

What did Joseph notice about the prisoners? (vs. 6) _____

Do you notice when others are having a bad day?_____

What do you usually do about it? _____

(By the way, Joseph must NOT have been sad himself if he confronted others.) Read verses 8-20. After hearing the dreams, Joseph shared good news to the butler—he was going to be delivered. But to the baker, Joseph had to tell some tough stuff. We must be willing to share with our friends both the good and the tough. God is good and forgiving—but He is also just and promises to judge sin. What should you tell others about...

sin: _____

forgiveness: _____

heaven: _____

hell: _____

Love others enough to tell them the truth—the whole truth of God's Word. Share God's love and warn of God's judgment. **Be a servant!**

Saturday and Sunday Review

Today and tomorrow, go back to each day's study and slowly re-read each question and answer. After reading and meditating on each day's principles, in the spaces provided write out what you learned and how you want God to use it to help you have the character and integrity of Joseph.

Monday

Joseph's Pit in the Desert
Genesis 37:13-35

_____
_____
_____
_____
_____
_____
_____
_____
_____

Tuesday

All Eyes Were On Joseph!
Genesis 39:1-23

_____
_____
_____
_____
_____
_____
_____
_____
_____

LET'S MEET POOR, PITIFUL MRS. POTIPHAR!
GENESIS 39:6-23

JOSEPH FACES TEMPTATION HEAD-ON!
GENESIS 39:6-23

JOSEPH DOES TIME IN PRISON!
GENESIS 39:20-40:23

Introduction to Week Four
Joseph: A Leader in Egypt

Joseph was 17 when he was sold by his brothers as a slave into Egypt, and in our study he is just about to end his prison time. For the next 13 years God continued to mold and shape Joseph to be the leader he was meant to be. It is interesting that some of the greatest leaders in the Bible spent many, many years serving others: Joseph served Potiphar and the prison guard; Joshua served Moses for forty years; David served his father and his king before he became king; our Lord Jesus Christ came to earth to serve, not to be served, and He is now sitting at the right hand of God. Most of our greatest Bible heroes were some of the greatest servants that ever lived. We are never more Christlike than when we are serving.

Spiritual leadership is a result of many years of growing and changing. Never give up or quit—never throw in the dirty towel. If you and your friends would be willing to learn life's lessons through years of serving others, you too will be able to experience years of being used by God to impact others for eternity. What you are learning through your teens and twenties will help you help others draw closer to the Lord in your forties and fifties.

This weeks' study will also deal with one of the enemies of becoming a successful spiritual leader—bitterness and lack of forgiveness. Humanly speaking, Joseph had every right to be angry and upset with his brothers, but he chose not to be. Like Joseph, spiritual leaders that God uses in a great way deal with past offences and hardships in a loving, forgiving, biblical way. Follow Joseph's example in discernment, wisdom, forgiveness, and love. Be a leader that will impact others and please God.

THE COWS AND THE CORN
GENESIS 41:1-32

Read about the Egyptian Pharaoh's dream in Genesis 41:1-32. How long had Joseph been stuck in prison before the butler finally remembered him? (vs. 1) _____

Two full years! We usually want to get out of our trials rather than go through them. How long have you been in a particular trial?

_____

We often complain when we are faced with a trial that continues for days and even weeks, but what about others who are in the midst of suffering for months and even years. Either way, in comparison to eternity, how does 2 Corinthians 4:17 describe our trials?

_____

_____

Pharaoh dreamed a dream. God used dreams and visions to communicate His Word in the early days of civilization. He has since given us His written Word to follow which is sufficient for all our needs. Verse 8 tells us that Pharaoh's spirit was troubled. God's Word often **troubles** individuals through conviction. When was the last time your heart was troubled because of something you were confronted with in God's Word?

_____

How did you deal with that **troubling**? _____

_____

Isn't it great to know that God both knows our future and is concerned about our provision and protection. God shared with Joseph and Pharaoh what was to happen in the next 14 years. Joseph lived a life of total faith in God for those seven years without visible proof of the future.

Don't you wish we had the faith of Joseph, whose faith was based on a king's dream of fat cows and skinny ears of corn? We have the actual holy, written Word of God. We too must accept by faith that what God tells us and warns us of in the future, will come! What about your future, or the future of the world, bothers you or causes you to worry or even be afraid? _____

Is God pleased when we worry, fret, and forget to trust in Him? _____

What does Philippians 4:6 say about worry? _____

_____

Try to write the message of Matthew 6:25-33 in one sentence. _____

_____

_____

What did Joseph make sure Pharaoh understood in Genesis 41:16? _____

_____

Joseph's answer was filled with humility and integrity. Joseph, because of his God-given gift to interpret dreams, could have milked this one (sorry for the pun) to get released from prison. He could have bartered and begged his way to a brand new life. But Joseph refused to take credit for something that was God's doing. He simply said, "It is not in me, but God, Jehovah God, not an Egyptian god, but the one and only true God can help you, Pharaoh." God used the dreams to get Pharaoh's attention; then He used Joseph to get Pharaoh's attention on the one true God. How has God used your life to draw a friend's, family member's, or co-worker's attention toward Himself?

_____

_____

Remember, your walk talks and your talk talks, but your walk talks much louder than your talk talks. Give an example of someone you know whose "walk" does not match up with his "talk." _____

How often adults compromise their relationship with God to keep a good job or "overlook" sin for a promotion! Teens do the same thing in order to be accepted by peers. They hide the fact that God is a part of their lives. They do not want their "Christianity" to hinder their popularity or fun. Joseph was concerned that Pharaoh knew it was JEHOVAH GOD who got all the credit. We too often do things to get ourselves noticed and forget that any talent we might have is a gift of God. When you play the piano or an instrument in church, who should get the praise?

_____

When you speak in a Sunday school class, who should get the credit?

_____

When you lead a soul to the Lord, who should receive the glory?

_____

Who does Colossians 1:16-18 teach should get the preeminence?

_____

What was John the Baptist's ministry philosophy found in John 3:27-31?

_____

When we seek to get personal glory or take all the credit for our accomplishments, we better beware of the awful sin of selfish pride. What do the following verses warn and teach about selfish **pride**?

Proverbs 13:10 _____

Proverbs 16:18 _____

James 4:6 _____

Learn from Joseph. Trust God for the future and give Him the glory!

FEAST OR FAMINE
GENESIS 41:33-52

Slowly read Genesis 41:33-52. When Joseph shared God's interpretation of the dreams and what needed to be done to prepare for the future, Pharaoh immediately chose Joseph to take charge because he was discreet and wise. Discreet and wise means to be cunning, intelligent, perceptive, and understanding. Where does true, godly wisdom come from according to James 1:5? _____

List the seven attributes of true wisdom found in James 3:17. _____

_____

_____

How many of these wise attributes do you see in your life? _____

What kind of man was Pharaoh looking for in verse 38? _____

_____

There are many ways for people to know that the Spirit of God dwells in us as Christians. According to Galatians 5:16, what will be evident if we walk in the spirit?

_____

_____

What will be seen in our lives when the Holy Spirit of God is in control of our lives? (Galatians 5:22-23) _____

_____

It was obvious that Pharaoh, Potiphar, and others must have seen some of these characteristics in Joseph's life. Go back and read Pharaoh's description of his dream in Genesis 41:17-24. What is a **kine**? _____

If you said a cow or cattle you are right. How may fat cows and good ears of corn were mentioned? _____ How many emaciated cows and thin ears of corn were mentioned? _____ In your own words, write out Joseph's interpretation of Pharaoh's dream. (Genesis 41:25-32) _____

_____

_____

Seven years of FEAST and seven years of FAMINE. God gave Joseph the wisdom to know how to manage during the good years of plenty in order to make it through the difficult years of famine. Even in our wealthy society today, we can learn some great lessons in managing the money we do have in order to be prepared for the future. It is interesting that Joseph knew that for seven years the Egyptians could live on just one-fifth—twenty percent—of their income. Since that was true, it had to have been that without the mandatory "savings account program" there would have been great waste.

What does God think about being **wasteful** in the following verses?

Proverbs 18:9 _____

Luke 15:13-14 _____

What does God say about **saving** ahead for harder times?

Proverbs 6:6-8 _____

Proverbs 10:4-5 _____

1 Timothy 6:17-19 _____

Joseph never let the pit, the prison, or the palace keep his focus off his God. The result for Joseph was a very important and powerful position under the Pharaoh of Egypt. Whether it is our circumstances in life or finances, we all will experience FEAST or FAMINE. Keep your focus!

The way we handle our money tells much about our hearts. Does money burn a hole in your pocket until you spend it? _____

Are you an impulsive shopper? _____

Do you hoard your money as a Christmas Scrooge and refuse to give any away?

_____

Do you waste all your money on games and entertainment? _____

Do you have a consistent savings plan? _____

Do you give a portion of the money you make to the Lord? _____

Do you have a goal in life to be rich? _____

Are you so lazy you would rather sleep than work? _____

Would God be pleased with the way you handle your money, savings, giving, and spending?

_____

What needs to change? _____

The Amish man said, "Show me what thou dost need, and I will show thee how to live without it!" A great biblical view of money and savings is found in Proverbs 30:8-9, **Remove far from me vanity and lies: give me neither poverty nor riches; feed me with food convenient for me: lest I be full, and deny thee, and say, Who is the LORD? or lest I be poor, and steal, and take the name of my God in vain.** Explain what these verses are teaching.

_____

_____

_____

You will need to determine how you will handle your money, but here is a simple budget that works well:

GIVING—20%…SAVINGS—20%…LIVING—60%.

We should pray, "Lord, just meet my needs…not too much and not too little. Help me to depend on You and be wise with what You give me."

WAKING UP A SLEEPING CONSCIENCE
GENESIS 42, 43, 44

To gain a good understanding of how God used Joseph to wake up a sleeping conscience in his brothers, take the time to read all three chapters: Genesis 42, 43, and 44. Since Joseph was 17 when he was sold into slavery and now 30 and second in command of all Egypt, how many years had Joseph's brothers covered their sin?

_____

Joseph's brothers agreed to sell Joseph (which was a death sentence in itself) and agreed to lie to their dad causing incredible heartache and grief. What does Genesis 37:31-35 say Jacob refused?

_____

Did Joseph's brothers seem to care whether their own father mourned and grieved?

_____

Did the boys seem at all convicted when they threw Joseph in the pit to die as a trapped animal? (Genesis 37:24-25) _____

Write out Genesis 42:21. _____

_____

_____

Anger, envy, selfishness, hypocrisy, and lying all work together to harden a conscience. It gets to the place where the heart is so seared it is past feeling. What does 1 Timothy 4:2 say about our conscience? _____

_____

According to Ephesians 4:19, what is the result of being past feeling?

_____

Search your heart. Is there any sin in the past or present that you have hidden and would be horrified if mom, dad, or any friends found out? Is there anything that you have covered so long it does not seem that bad anymore? What does Proverbs 28:13 say about covering sin? _____

_____

God was using Joseph to "wake up the sleeping consciences" in his brothers. A "sleeping" or seared conscience is a scorched, hardened, insensible conscience that is insensitive to God and His standards for our behavior. Here are two methods God used on Joseph's brothers.

1. God wakes up a sleeping conscience by making us victims of unfair treatment we once gave others.

2. God wakes up a sleeping conscience by giving us undeserved expressions of His love and grace.

GOD USED JOSEPH TO WAKE UP THE SLEEPING CONSCIENCES OF HIS BROTHERS BY MAKING THEM VICTIMS OF UNFAIR TREATMENT THEY ONCE GAVE JOSEPH.

Joseph called them spies. (42:9) - They called him a spy. (37:2, 18)

Joseph spoke roughly. (42:7) - They spoke roughly to him. (37:4)

Joseph put them in a prison. (42:17) - They put him into a PIT. (37:23-24)

Simeon was kept in Egypt. (42:19-24) - Joseph was sold to Egypt. (37:27-28)

Joseph gave Benjamin favor. (43:34) - Jacob showed Joseph favor! (37:3)

If you plant tomato seeds, what will grow? _____

If you plant a kernel of corn, how much corn will grow? _____

What does Galatians 6:7 say about sowing and reaping? _____

Is it possible that some of the difficulties you are now facing are a direct result of past sin that has not been dealt with in a biblical way? _____

Has anyone been mean or unkind to you? _____

Can you think of three individuals that you have been mean and unkind to?

_____

Have you ever done something for someone and received no thanks for your effort?

_____

When was the last time you wrote a thank you note to anyone? _____

_____

Write out what is called the "Golden Rule" which is taken from Matthew 7:12. _____

_____

GOD USED JOSEPH TO WAKE UP THE SLEEPING CONSCIENCES OF HIS BROTHERS BY GIVING THEM UNDESERVED EXPRESSIONS OF LOVE, FORGIVENESS, AND KINDNESS.

To the same brothers who hated him and wanted him dead, Joseph showed FORGIVENESS! Write out Genesis 50:19. _____

_____

To the same brothers who threw him in a pit and sold him into slavery, Joseph gave COMFORT! Write out Genesis 50:21._____

_____

To the same brothers who could not speak peaceably with him and could not have cared less about him, Joseph showed KINDNESS! Write out Genesis 50:20. _____

_____

Has anyone who you have been mean or uncaring to done something nice for you? How does that make you feel? That is what God does for us every day of our lives. We deserve nothing, and yet God gives us forgiveness, mercy, and His blessing. The goodness of God should encourage us to love Him more and hate sin more. Will we?

A FAMILY REUNION
GENESIS 45

One of the most dramatic scenes in all Scripture is found in Genesis 45. This chapter cannot be read without experiencing the shock and fear of the brothers and the joy and tears of Joseph. Slowly read through Genesis 45 before you continue this study. One of the most emotion-filled verses is Genesis 45:3.

And Joseph said unto his brethren, I am Joseph; doth my father yet live? And his brethren could not answer him; for they were troubled at his presence.

Of course the brothers were troubled at his presence! Who wouldn't be? The one person who knew about their covered sin stood before them full of power and prestige. I would not stop at troubled, I would have been scared to death! They were caught red-handed! There was no way they could lie their way out of this one. How do you think Reuben, Simeon, Judah, and the rest of the brothers felt inside?_____

_____

Has your mom or dad ever caught you in a lie? How did it feel? _____

_____

Could you imagine how it would feel if you plopped down at the computer after school to check some scores or prices, got tempted to hit a couple of Internet sites that were wicked, only to look behind you and see mom standing in the doorway with tears running down her cheeks? How would mom feel? _____

_____

How would the one that was caught feel? _____

Now we know a little bit better how we make God feel every day. What do the following verses say about hiding our sin from God?

Proverbs 5:21 _____

Proverbs 15:3 _____

Psalm 94:7-11 _____

Just as Joseph's brothers stood before the one and only one who knew about their sin and had the power to punish such wickedness, so we will someday stand before a holy, sin-hating God. According to Philippians 2:9-11, what will all men someday do?

_____

_____

When Joseph revealed who he was to his brothers, he immediately tried to calm and comfort their hearts by his next few statements. **Now therefore be not grieved, nor angry with yourselves, that ye sold me hither: for God did send me before you to preserve life.** (45:5) Who did Joseph say was ultimately responsible for his being in Egypt?

_____

_____

What did Joseph tell his brothers they should NOT feel? _____

_____

According to Genesis 45:5 and 7, why was Joseph content with God's plan for his life? Why did God allow Joseph to be sold into Egypt? _____

_____

There are two major lessons we can learn from this family reunion.

1. Families should not allow the sins and hardships of the past to continue, but should offer true forgiveness and reconciliation.

2. God has a sovereign plan for each one of our lives.

Families should forgive. Are there any harsh words, outbursts of anger, cruel actions, unkind words, abusive behavior, or selfish wickedness in your family "memories" that have never been handled with biblical forgiveness and restoration? Many families are not close and the family relationships are incredibly shallow. Joseph was willing to forgive. Are you? If we refuse to forgive others, what does God promise in Matthew 6:14-15?

_____

_____

God is sovereign: Ron Hamilton, alias Patch the Pirate, wrote a song right after he learned he had cancer in his eye entitled, *Rejoice in the Lord*. The first verse is written below; fill in the chorus if you know it.

> ### "GOD NEVER MOVES WITHOUT PURPOSE OR PLAN,
> ### WHEN TRYING A SERVANT AND MOLDING A MAN;
> ### GIVE THANKS TO THE LORD, THOUGH YOUR TESTING SEEMS LONG;
> ### IN DARKNESS HE GIVETH A SONG."

_____

_____

When we truly believe that God is all-knowing and all-powerful, it is so much easier to face the hardships of life. Allow the following passages to comfort your heart as you meditate on God's almighty power.

Psalm 23 _____

Psalm 27 _____

Psalm 57 _____

Psalm 91 _____

Remember, families should forgive and God is sovereign.

A Picture of True Forgiveness
Genesis 50

The last ten chapters of Genesis describe God's plan in using Joseph to keep His people and many others from dying because of the great famine. Joseph interprets Pharaoh's dream in chapter 41, tests his brothers in chapters 42-45, watches his family settle in Egypt in chapters 46-47, and receives Jacob's blessing in chapters 48-49. Genesis 50 describes Jacob's death and burial, Joseph's forgiveness, and Joseph's death. All through these chapters we see Joseph realize that "God is with me."

Joseph was a remarkable man. Where he offered forgiveness to his brothers, Mrs. Potiphar, and the forgetful butler, most of us would have cried, "REVENGE!" Where Joseph promised to take care of his brothers and their families, many would have said, "You wanted nothing to do with me…now I want nothing to do with you!" Joseph was a forgiving man. Please read Genesis 45:1-28 and Genesis 50:14-26. Joseph exhibited three aspects of forgiveness. Understanding forgiveness is a choice.

CHOOSE NOT TO SEEK REVENGE!

God has much to say about vengeance. Remember in our first week of study we looked at Simeon and Levi in Genesis 34? How did they handle the sin against their sister Dinah? _____

_____

Today we wouldn't take swords and destroy a whole city, but we do use our tongues to cut and hurt as much as possible. From Romans 12:17-21, list at least five ways to avoid "taking revenge."

> **Recompense to no man evil for evil. Provide things honest in the sight of all men. If it be possible, as much as lieth in you, live peaceably with all men. Dearly beloved, avenge not yourselves, but rather give place unto wrath: for it is written, Vengeance is mine; I will repay, saith the Lord. Therefore if thine enemy hunger, feed him; if he thirst, give him drink: for in so doing thou shalt heap coals of fire on his head. Be not overcome of evil, but overcome evil with good.**

_____

_____

Instead of playing "gotcha last," what five things should we do according to 1 Peter 3:8?

_____

_____

CHOOSE TO DO GOOD!

Fill in the blanks: Matthew 5:44: **But I say unto you, _____ your enemies, _____ them that curse you, do _____ to them that hate you, and _____ for them which despitefully use you, and persecute you.**

When someone is angry with you, the best way to diffuse that anger is by kindness. What stirs up strife? (Proverbs 10:12) _____

What kind of answer turns away wrath? (Proverbs 15:1) _____

When someone says something mean to you, what should you say back to them?

_____

When someone hates you and calls you ugly names, how should you reply?

_____

Proverbs 25:21-22 promises the Lord will reward whom? _____

_____

Choose to Forgive!

**Forgiveness means I will never bring it up to you,
to myself or to anyone else again.**

Is there anyone on this earth that you refuse to forgive? How many times does
Matthew 18:21-22 tell us to forgive others? _____

(By the way, Christ is actually emphasizing that there is no limit to forgiveness.)
Luke 23:34, which shows our Lord's forgiving heart, is one of the most powerful verses
on forgiveness in the whole Bible. Read the verse and explain the context of this
passage. _____

_____

_____

In your own words, what does the phrase in Ephesians 4:26, **Let not the sun go down
upon your wrath** mean? _____

_____

When we refuse to forgive, a spiritual cancer creeps into our hearts—a cancer called
bitterness. What does Ephesians 4:31 tell us to do with **bitterness**?

_____

Once we seek forgiveness for our bitterness, Ephesians 4:32 tells us to replace it with
kindness, compassion, and forgiveness. In that verse, what is the pattern of forgiveness
that we should follow? _____

_____

Have your sins been forgiven? _____

Write out a brief testimony of your salvation experience when you experienced
complete forgiveness of all your sins. _____

_____

_____

Let's forgive others just like our Lord forgave us. Thank you, Lord.

Saturday and Sunday Review

Today and tomorrow, go back to each day's study and slowly re-read each question and answer. After reading and meditating on each day's principles, in the spaces provided write out what you learned and how you want God to use it to help you have the character and integrity of Joseph.

MONDAY

THE COWS AND THE CORN
GENESIS 41:1-32

_____

_____

_____

_____

_____

_____

_____

_____

_____

TUESDAY

FEAST OR FAMINE
GENESIS 41:33-52

_____

_____

_____

_____

_____

_____

_____

_____

_____

WAKING UP A SLEEPING CONSCIENCE
GENESIS 42, 43, 44

A FAMILY REUNION
GENESIS 45

A PICTURE OF TRUE FORGIVENESS
GENESIS 50

Introduction to Week Five
Joseph: A Type of Christ

Our approach to this week's study will be quite different than the first four weeks. Each day we will examine four characteristics of Joseph's life that are typical of Jesus' life. Even though Joseph lived centuries before Jesus Christ walked on earth as a man, Joseph's intense desire to focus on the presence of God and passion to please God gave evidence of many of these characteristics of Jesus Christ. Joseph, unknowingly, actually followed the admonition of Paul in Romans 13:14.

**BUT PUT YE ON THE LORD JESUS CHRIST,
AND MAKE NOT PROVISION FOR THE FLESH,
TO FULFIL THE LUSTS THEREOF.**

We are all encouraged to put on the characteristics of Christ—to be like Christ! Everything that happens in life is for a reason and a purpose. Again the Apostle Paul reminds us of this in Romans 8:28-29.

**AND WE KNOW THAT ALL THINGS WORK TOGETHER FOR GOOD
TO THEM THAT LOVE GOD, TO THEM WHO ARE THE CALLED
ACCORDING TO HIS PURPOSE. FOR WHOM HE DID FOREKNOW,
HE ALSO DID PREDESTINATE TO BE CONFORMED
TO THE IMAGE OF HIS SON,
THAT HE MIGHT BE THE FIRSTBORN AMONG MANY BRETHREN.**

The Old Testament is filled with pictures and illustrations that point towards our Lord Jesus Christ. Many of the situations and circumstances that Joseph faced were typical of what Jesus Christ was to face on earth. Joseph is what is called a "type" of Christ. As we study his life, we see many similarities that appear in the life of Christ. Our circumstances in life are usually unchangeable, but our character is often produced by choosing to please God rather than self. As Joseph's life reminds us of Jesus' life, may our families and friends say the same of our lives. Live in such a way that others see Jesus Christ in you.

CHANGED TO CHRISTLIKENESS - PART 1

NOTE: Please read the passages listed under each statement below and meditate on the similarities between Jesus and Joseph. Then, in the spaces provided, carefully explain what they had in common and how it can affect our lives today. Some will be easier to explain than others. Enjoy your study as we learn how to be more like Christ.

BOTH JESUS AND JOSEPH WERE GREATLY LOVED.
JOSEPH: Genesis 37:1-4
JESUS: Matthew 3:17 • John 3:35 • John 5:19-20
John 15:8-12 • John 17:21-26

_____
_____
_____
_____
_____
_____
_____
_____
_____
_____

BOTH JESUS AND JOSEPH WERE EXTREMELY HATED.
JOSEPH: Genesis 37:4-11
JESUS: John 1:10-11 • Isaiah 53:3 • Luke 20:13-14
John 3:31-32 • Acts 7:51

_____
_____
_____
_____
_____
_____
_____
_____
_____
_____

BOTH JESUS AND JOSEPH WERE SHEPHERDS.

JOSEPH: Genesis 37:1-17
JESUS: John 10:1-18 • Matthew 9:36 • Hebrew 13:20
1 Peter 2:25 • 1 Peter 5:4

_____

_____

_____

_____

_____

_____

_____

_____

_____

_____

_____

_____

BOTH JESUS AND JOSEPH WERE SENT OUT BY LOVING FATHERS.

JOSEPH: Genesis 37:13-14
JESUS: Matthew 10:40 • Luke 4:18 • Luke 9:48 • John 5:23-24
John 6:37-40 • John 6:44 • John 8:42 • John 20:21

_____

_____

_____

_____

_____

_____

_____

_____

_____

_____

_____

_____

CHANGED TO CHRISTLIKENESS - PART 2

NOTE: Please read the passages listed under each statement below and meditate on the similarities between Jesus and Joseph. Then, in the spaces provided, carefully explain what they had in common and how it can affect our lives today. Some will be easier to explain than others. Enjoy your study as we learn how to be more like Christ.

THERE WERE SOME WHO WANTED TO KILL BOTH JESUS AND JOSEPH.

JOSEPH: Genesis 37:18-20

JESUS: John 7:1 • Mark 15:12-14 • John 5:15-18

John 11:7-16 • John 19:5-6

_____

_____

_____

_____

_____

_____

_____

_____

_____

_____

BOTH JESUS AND JOSEPH WERE SOLD AS SLAVES FOR SILVER.

JOSEPH: Genesis 37:24-28 • Psalm 105:17 • Acts 7:9

JESUS: Matthew 26:14-16 • Matthew 27:1-10 • Leviticus 27:3-7

_____

_____

_____

_____

_____

_____

_____

_____

_____

_____

BOTH JESUS AND JOSEPH WERE EXEMPLARY SERVANTS.

JOSEPH: Genesis 39:1-6 • Genesis 39:19-23
JESUS: Philippians 2:5-8 • Mark 10:45 • Luke 22:26-27 • John 13:1-17

BOTH JESUS AND JOSEPH PLEASED THEIR MASTERS WELL.

JOSEPH: Genesis 39:1-6 • Genesis 41:37-46
JESUS: Matthew 3:16-17 • Matthew 17:1-5 • 2 Peter 1:16-18

CHANGED TO CHRISTLIKENESS - PART 3

NOTE: Please read the passages listed under each statement below and meditate on the similarities between Jesus and Joseph. Then, in the spaces provided, carefully explain what they had in common and how it can affect our lives today. Some will be easier to explain than others. Enjoy your study as we learn how to be more like Christ.

BOTH JESUS AND JOSEPH WERE SORELY TEMPTED.
JOSEPH: Genesis 39:6-23
JESUS: Matthew 4:1-11 • Hebrews 2:17-18 • Hebrews 4:14-16

_____

_____

_____

_____

_____

_____

_____

_____

_____

BOTH JESUS AND JOSEPH WERE FALSELY ACCUSED.
JOSEPH: Genesis 39:6-23
JESUS: John 18:38-19:6 • Luke 23:39-41
Matthew 27:3-4 • 1 Peter 1:18-19

_____

_____

_____

_____

_____

_____

_____

_____

_____

Both Jesus and Joseph, although innocent, suffered severely.

JOSEPH: Genesis 37:18-28 • Genesis 39:20-40:23

JESUS: Isaiah 53:1-12 • Psalm 22 • John 19:1-42

_____

_____

_____

_____

_____

_____

_____

_____

_____

_____

_____

_____

_____

_____

_____

Both Jesus and Joseph were numbered with transgressors.

JOSEPH: Genesis 39:19-20

JESUS: Isaiah 53:12 • Mark 15:27-32 • Hebrews 12:2-4

_____

_____

_____

_____

_____

_____

_____

_____

_____

_____

_____

_____

_____

_____

CHANGED TO CHRISTLIKENESS - PART 4

NOTE: Please read the passages listed under each statement below and meditate on the similarities between Jesus and Joseph. Then, in the spaces provided, carefully explain what they had in common and how it can affect our lives today. Some will be easier to explain than others. Enjoy your study as we learn how to be more like Christ.

BOTH JESUS AND JOSEPH WON THE RESPECT OF THEIR JAILORS.
JOSEPH: Genesis 39:20-23 • Genesis 40:1-4
JESUS: John 19:1-6 • Matthew 27:54 • Mark 15:39 • Luke 23:47

_____

_____

_____

_____

_____

_____

_____

_____

_____

_____

BOTH JESUS AND JOSEPH PROMISED BLESSING TO ONE CRIMINAL AND JUDGMENT TO THE OTHER.
JOSEPH: Genesis 40:5-23
JESUS: Luke 23:32-43 • Isaiah 53:12

_____

_____

_____

_____

_____

_____

_____

_____

_____

BOTH JESUS AND JOSEPH WERE FREED FROM BONDAGE AND EXALTED TO A THRONE.

JOSEPH: Genesis 41:14-57
JESUS: Mark 16:19 • Acts 7:54-56 • Romans 8:34 • Philippians 2:7-11
Colossians 3:1 • Hebrews 10:12 • 1 Peter 3:22

_____

_____

_____

_____

_____

_____

_____

_____

_____

_____

_____

_____

_____

BOTH JESUS AND JOSEPH FORETOLD GOD'S FUTURE PLANS.

JOSEPH: Genesis 37:5-11 • Genesis 40:8-23 • Genesis 41:15-32
JESUS: John 2:19-22 • John 3:14 • John 14:1-3 • Luke 23:43 • John 3:16

_____

_____

_____

_____

_____

_____

_____

_____

_____

_____

_____

_____

_____

_____

CHANGED TO CHRISTLIKENESS - PART 5

NOTE: Please read the passages listed under each statement below and meditate on the similarities between Jesus and Joseph. Then, in the spaces provided, carefully explain what they had in common and how it can affect our lives today. Some will be easier to explain than others. Enjoy your study as we learn how to be more like Christ.

BOTH JESUS AND JOSEPH WERE USED BY GOD TO SAVE MANY LIVES.

JOSEPH: Genesis 45:5-8 • Genesis 50:19-21

JESUS: John 3:16 • 1 John 4:10 • Romans 5:6-10 • 1 Timothy 1:15-16

_____

_____

_____

_____

_____

_____

_____

_____

_____

_____

BOTH JESUS AND JOSEPH OFFERED FULL FORGIVENESS TO THEIR LOVED ONES WHO MISTREATED THEM.

JOSEPH: Genesis 50:15-21

JESUS: 1 John 1:4-10 • Romans 8:1 • Titus 2:13-14

Ephesians 4:32 • Colossians 1:14

_____

_____

_____

_____

_____

_____

_____

_____

_____

_____

BOTH JESUS AND JOSEPH WILLINGLY ACCEPTED GOD'S WILL FOR THE GOOD OF OTHERS, EVEN THOUGH IT WAS VERY HARD TO ACCEPT.

JOSEPH: Genesis 45:5-7 • Genesis 50:19-21

JESUS: Luke 22:41-44 • John 6:38-40 • John 8:28-29 • John 16:7

_____

_____

_____

_____

_____

_____

_____

_____

_____

_____

_____

_____

_____

_____

BOTH JESUS AND JOSEPH ARE IN HEAVEN TODAY.

JOSEPH: Genesis 50:22-26 • 2 Corinthians 5:8

JESUS: John 14:1-3 • John 16:7-16 • Acts 1:9-11 • Acts 7:55-60

_____

_____

_____

_____

_____

_____

_____

_____

_____

_____

_____

_____

_____

_____

Saturday and Sunday Review

Today and tomorrow, go back to each day's study and slowly re-read each question and answer. After reading and meditating on each day's principles, in the spaces provided write out what you learned and how you want God to use it to help you have the character and integrity of Joseph.

Monday

BOTH JESUS AND JOSEPH WERE GREATLY LOVED.
BOTH JESUS AND JOSEPH WERE EXTREMELY HATED.
BOTH JESUS AND JOSEPH WERE SHEPHERDS.
BOTH JESUS AND JOSEPH WERE SENT OUT BY LOVING FATHERS.

_____

_____

_____

_____

_____

_____

_____

_____

Tuesday

THERE WERE THOSE WHO WANTED TO KILL BOTH JESUS AND JOSEPH.
BOTH JESUS AND JOSEPH WERE SOLD AS SLAVES FOR SILVER.
BOTH JESUS AND JOSEPH WERE EXEMPLARY SERVANTS.
BOTH JESUS AND JOSEPH PLEASED THEIR MASTERS WELL.

_____

_____

_____

_____

_____

_____

_____

_____

WEDNESDAY

BOTH JESUS AND JOSEPH WERE SORELY TEMPTED.

BOTH JESUS AND JOSEPH WERE FALSELY ACCUSED.

BOTH JESUS AND JOSEPH, ALTHOUGH INNOCENT, SUFFERED SEVERELY.

BOTH JESUS AND JOSEPH WERE NUMBERED WITH TRANSGRESSORS.

_____

_____

_____

_____

_____

THURSDAY

BOTH JESUS AND JOSEPH WON THE RESPECT OF THEIR JAILORS.

BOTH JESUS AND JOSEPH PROMISED BLESSING TO ONE CRIMINAL AND JUDGMENT TO THE OTHER.

BOTH JESUS AND JOSEPH WERE FREED FROM BONDAGE AND EXALTED TO A THRONE.

BOTH JESUS AND JOSEPH FORETOLD GOD'S FUTURE PLANS.

_____

_____

_____

_____

_____

FRIDAY

BOTH JESUS AND JOSEPH WERE USED BY GOD TO SAVE MANY LIVES.

BOTH JESUS AND JOSEPH OFFERED FULL FORGIVENESS TO THEIR LOVED ONES WHO MISTREATED THEM.

BOTH JESUS AND JOSEPH WILLINGLY ACCEPTED GOD'S WILL FOR THE GOOD OF OTHERS, EVEN THOUGH IT WAS VERY HARD TO ACCEPT.

BOTH JESUS AND JOSEPH ARE IN HEAVEN TODAY.

_____

_____

_____

_____

_____

Introduction to Week Six
A Review of Joseph's Life

Read. Memorize. Meditate. Review. Read. Memorize. Meditate. Review. Read. Memorize. Meditate. Review. Read. Memorize. Meditate. Review. Read. Memorize. Meditate. Review. Read. Memorize. Meditate. Review.

Get the idea? In our fast-paced, no-time-to-stop-and-eat world, we must take time to review, or the truths will have a difficult time sinking into our minds and lives. We've spent five weeks closely studying one of the greatest Bible heroes in Scripture.

Joseph was a man of character! He came from a difficult family, was hated, abused, and sold off as a slave to die. He was falsely accused and unfairly imprisoned. He was forgotten!

But he never took his focus off God and His promises. Joseph was a Patriarch who received special revelation from God just like his father Jacob, his grandfather Isaac, and his great-grandfather Abraham. Joseph chose to believe God and was rewarded for it.

As we spend our last week reviewing what we have learned for the past five weeks, I trust that these truths will become such a major part of our lives that people will remember us just like they remember Joseph—a type of Christ.

May we follow the pattern of our Lord and Savior Jesus Christ and set a pattern for others to follow. Enjoy your review.

REVIEW OF JOSEPH'S FAMILY ALBUM

MONDAY

A SNAPSHOT OF JOSEPH'S FATHER: JACOB
GENESIS 25 AND 27

_____

_____

_____

_____

_____

_____

_____

_____

_____

_____

_____

TUESDAY

A SNAPSHOT OF JOSEPH'S MOTHER: RACHEL
GENESIS 29-30

_____

_____

_____

_____

_____

_____

_____

_____

_____

_____

_____

_____

A SNAPSHOT OF JOSEPH'S BROTHER: REUBEN
GENESIS 29:32; 35:22; 37:21-26; 42:20-22; 49:1-4

_____
_____
_____
_____
_____
_____
_____
_____

THURSDAY

A SNAPSHOT OF JOSEPH'S BROTHERS: SIMEON & LEVI
GENESIS 34:1-31; 49:5-7

_____
_____
_____
_____
_____
_____
_____
_____

FRIDAY

A SNAPSHOT OF JOSEPH'S BROTHER: JUDAH
GENESIS 38:1-30

_____
_____
_____
_____
_____
_____
_____
_____

Review of Joseph's Early Years

Tattletale or Truth-Teller
Genesis 37

_____
_____
_____
_____
_____
_____
_____
_____
_____
_____
_____
_____
_____

Tuesday

"Dad always liked you best!"
Genesis 37

_____
_____
_____
_____
_____
_____
_____
_____
_____
_____
_____
_____

DREAMER OF DREAMS
GENESIS 37:5-11

_____
_____
_____
_____
_____
_____
_____
_____

SIBLING RIVALRY AT ITS WORST
GENESIS 37

_____
_____
_____
_____
_____
_____
_____
_____

OBEDIENCE: QUICKLY, SWEETLY, AND COMPLETELY
GENESIS 37:12-17

_____
_____
_____
_____
_____
_____
_____
_____

Review of Joseph: Seventeen to Thirty

Joseph's Pit in the Desert
Genesis 37:13-35

_____
_____
_____
_____
_____
_____
_____
_____
_____
_____
_____
_____

Tuesday

All Eyes Were on Joseph!
Genesis 39:1-23

_____
_____
_____
_____
_____
_____
_____
_____
_____
_____
_____

LET'S MEET POOR, PITIFUL MRS. POTIPHAR!
GENESIS 39:6-23

JOSEPH FACES TEMPTATION HEAD-ON!
GENESIS 39:6-23

JOSEPH DOES TIME IN PRISON!
GENESIS 39:20-40:23

Review of Joseph: A Leader in Egypt

The Cows and the Corn
Genesis 41:1-32

_____

_____

_____

_____

_____

_____

_____

_____

_____

_____

_____

Tuesday

Feast or Famine
Genesis 41:33-52

_____

_____

_____

_____

_____

_____

_____

_____

_____

_____

_____

WAKING UP A SLEEPING CONSCIENCE
GENESIS 42, 43, 44

A FAMILY REUNION
GENESIS 45

A PICTURE OF TRUE FORGIVENESS
GENESIS 50

Review of Joseph: A Type of Christ

Monday

- Both Jesus and Joseph were greatly loved.
- Both Jesus and Joseph were extremely hated.
- Both Jesus and Joseph were shepherds.
- Both Jesus and Joseph were sent out by loving fathers.

_____
_____
_____
_____
_____
_____
_____
_____
_____
_____
_____

Tuesday

- There were those who wanted to kill both Jesus and Joseph.
- Both Jesus and Joseph were sold as slaves for silver.
- Both Jesus and Joseph were exemplary servants.
- Both Jesus and Joseph pleased their masters well.

_____
_____
_____
_____
_____
_____
_____
_____
_____
_____

WEDNESDAY

- BOTH JESUS AND JOSEPH WERE SORELY TEMPTED.
- BOTH JESUS AND JOSEPH WERE FALSELY ACCUSED.
- BOTH JESUS AND JOSEPH, ALTHOUGH INNOCENT, SUFFERED SEVERELY.
- BOTH JESUS AND JOSEPH WERE NUMBERED WITH TRANSGRESSORS.

_____
_____
_____
_____
_____
_____

THURSDAY

- BOTH JESUS AND JOSEPH WON THE RESPECT OF THEIR JAILORS.
- BOTH JESUS AND JOSEPH PROMISED BLESSING TO ONE CRIMINAL AND JUDGMENT TO THE OTHER.
- BOTH JESUS AND JOSEPH WERE FREED FROM BONDAGE AND EXALTED TO A THRONE.
- BOTH JESUS AND JOSEPH FORETOLD GOD'S FUTURE PLANS.

_____
_____
_____
_____
_____

FRIDAY

- BOTH JESUS AND JOSEPH WERE USED BY GOD TO SAVE MANY LIVES.
- BOTH JESUS AND JOSEPH OFFERED FULL FORGIVENESS TO THEIR LOVED ONES WHO MISTREATED THEM.
- BOTH JESUS AND JOSEPH WILLINGLY ACCEPTED GOD'S WILL FOR THE GOOD OF OTHERS, EVEN THOUGH IT WAS VERY HARD TO ACCEPT.
- BOTH JESUS AND JOSEPH ARE IN HEAVEN TODAY.

_____
_____
_____
_____
_____
_____